Tempest At Twilight

A Collection of Poems About Growing Into Consciousness

Imani J. Harrigan

BookLeaf Publishing

India | USA | UK

Made with ♥ on the BookLeaf Publishing Platform
www.bookleafpub.in
www.bookleafpub.com

Acknowledgment

Glory be to God, through Him, all things are possible. Without the support of my family, this book would not exist. Thank you, Mom and Baba, for always encouraging my writing from a young age. Thank you, big brothers, for listening to my work. I'm especially grateful for my brother Chez, who continuously told me—with the utmost certainty— that I would be a published writer one day.

Although my first educators were my family, I wouldn't be here without the English teachers over the years. Thank you, Mrs. Thomas, for always having a critical yet kind word about my writing. Thank you, Dr. Forkum, for encouraging me to love syntax. Thank you, Professor Mort, for inspiring me to test the bounds of my creativity. And thank you, to all the teachers who molded me.

Lastly, I'd like to thank my friends who lived through the whirlwind of strangeness while I

was creating this. They listened. They
attended my first poetry readings. They were
the most amazing friends I could ask for.
Thank you, Imani, Anna, Sneesha, and Nena.

Preface

First Corinthians 13:11 speaks of acting as a child until it is time to put childish things away. As a child, I dreamed of adulthood, where I would inherit the freedom to pursue imagination without limitations, without the word *no*. Turning the page into the rest of my life has been both unexpected and disappointing. Growing up doesn't grace children with freedom; instead, it erases and erodes castles of wonder for the practical and the responsible. As I grew up, my mind, body, and soul absorbed love, anguish, felicity, and understanding. Blossoming into the adult I am still becoming has been a journey both jarring and illuminating, but with each new day, I strive to authorize my own *yes* when the world distributes *no*.

Lovely Child

Clinking in this Mason Jar are white precious gems from the mouth of her love.
Held in a child's jaw for five to seven seasons emerging one or two at a time.

Surprising her with each smile from an innocent cherubic face.
Threaded between her forefingers brown strands softer than a lion's mane, as thick as tall grass stalks.

Whispers gently tickle young ears, *goodnight, my baby*.
Massaging repeatedly her offspring's head, *good morning, my baby*.

Caressing circles soothe small tummies, *feel better, my love*.
Kissing lightly mending childish booboos, *all better, love*.

Schoolhouse Blues

All is good and fair for eight hours in a square
where stampeding footsteps go
bye-bye in this holding cell.

Staggered yard hours a few blocks at a time
where stampeding footsteps form factions.

Gruel, served or paid, for it makes no
difference. A lack of nutrition advertised
behind a balanced diet is the mission.

Bells ring stampeding footsteps on probation,
to be picked up by their guardian parole
officer.

Birthrights & Birthmarks

See this skin, baby? It has a history.
Bequeathed to you from your daddy and me.
Given to us by your grandparents.
Born to them from your great-grandparents.
This beautiful caramel color traces miles.

Feel this skin, baby? Yours is smooth.
A trait we now have from a time when scars were
plenty. Strips here, raised flesh there,
bones protruding.
This beautiful caramel color tells a story.

Map this skin, baby? It reveals a home.
That birthmark there is in the shape of Africa
where our blood grew before it toiled this land.
You've been gifted a reminder of what their
forefathers stole from us.
This caramel color is evidence of their sin.

Elm Street

I was born prematurely in a hospital during
the morning. I was born to offset the trio of
boys.
I was born evicting us from their small
apartment, pregnant with too many children;
I was born the girl who had her own room in
our first home in 2005.

I grew up bent over
A pink and white toy box.

Pink and white toy box with baby dolls, with
Dora, with spines
        of destroyed books before I learned to
love them,
With childish adventure, with Satrapi's
stories.

Pink and white toy box with endless
imagination, with toys stolen
        from brothers such as Little Green
Soldiers,

with Disney princess stickers, Barbie dolls,
and pieces of different clothing fabrics.

I loved the word *play*.
Prized possession placed, perchance,
positioned
perfectly packed, painted pictures.

Parents prayed nightly.
Between the economy, four kids, and owning
two homes the years passed.

One day, it would be half a home.
It was a yellow house
Across from a vineyard

Foreclosed and yard sales,
Staked signs in the front yard.
That must have been in 2008.

Hopping homes haunted humans,
Harrowing humiliation hovered heavily.
I see the leftover house is where we live now.

I know the leftover house is where my
grandma died.
Pink and white toy box with no toys, with no
dolls, with no fashion designs—
Gone to storage.

Weekend Movie Night

Tonight's a twilight marathon!
Peek behind closed eyes as they kiss again, eye
roll.

Jacob or Edward, you choose?

Another birthday makes double digits come
true!
The piñata is busted!
Candy scattered across the backyard and into
the neighbor's yard.
Kids darting in and out of the jumping house.
Paper plates, chocolate cake, and silver plastic
spoons.
Autumn, wintertime, spring forward,
summer tan.

Dear God, look at you! No, look at you!

Changes here, changes there, changes
everywhere.
Wrinkles replace fat,

Sharp angles overtake cherubic faces.
A playhouse could never truly imitate real
life.
Forgotten so much,
Out of touch,
Old debts whispered secrets and unspoken
regrets.
Feeling guilty, but I'm the one who left.

Coveted Heart

How sweet to be coveted.
A pair of gloves
        preventing winter's chill.

How sweet to be owned.
A scarf
        thrust on like a noose.

How sweet to be kept safe.
A pair of boots
        washed, polished, and waxed.

How sweet on a shelf.
How sweet in the sheets.
        How sweet, a kept thing.

Mr. Clear Eyes

Bountiful, bouncing ringlets, voluminous
cyclic swirls,
rolling fertile grapevines,
jealous mahogany would be inspired by the
shade,
as soft as silk, but velvet is the best
descriptor,
a crown such as yours decrees a delicate
caress,
gentle care.

Tempestuous azure eyes, narrowed, steady,
and grave,
with silence a crystal blue,
harboring intelligence and intrigue,
one drowns in them, but you deploy
lifeboats,
a cocksure captain directing from the bow,
a pirate hoarding sapphires.

Falling further in assessment, deep dimples,
obscured by your austere snow facade,
revealed by a felicitous smile,

unveiled with the smallest upturn of your
cupid's bow,
it etches the evidence of tender memories
around your eyes,
a sight that arrives as an unfamiliar guest
visiting, but I know it as home.

Bitter Sweets

Ink stained. My hands are stained with ink,
colorful ink,

> *Did you know you've made me a writer?*

Pitchy notes. My notes are pitchy with woe,
reminiscent woe,

> *Did you know you've made me a singer?*

Warning eyes. My eyes are red with warning,
salty warning,

> *Did you know you've made me a weeper?*

Growing stiff. My limbs are stiff with winter,
many winters,

> *Did you know you've made me a*
spinster?

A writer, a singer, a weeper, a spinster—
You are an engineer.

Is It I'll Never Forget or Forgive?

As a little girl, I pondered
What is love?
Was it the waning warmth in my chest when my
mother kissed me? Or the weightlessness of sitting
atop my father's shoulders,
Feeling as tall as Everest?
Was it the dull ache turned into a sinking
sensation when my brother left for college? Or the
smell of coffee during the car ride home,
I hate coffee.

As a little girl, I picked apart flowers.
Was this petal "he loves me" or "he loves me not"?
Or was I a cheat?
Counting the petals beforehand, silently,
Loves me always, he does.

As a youth, I inquired.
Was it the first time we met? Or the first time we
fancied a game of Jenga?

*Was it the finite hours of battery wasted
experiencing each other through the phone? Or
interloping tears squeezed from a snapshot?*
Those snapshots of her.

As a weary soul, I ask myself what love is.
*Is it the numbness of loss keeping me up at night?
Or the night terrors parading as dreams?
Is it the obsession with who I'm meant to be? Or
the grueling suspicion he's not out of reach?
Is it the lingering attraction festering like an open
wound?*
Pus filled.
*Or is it my everlasting inability to separate me
from you?
Is love something I cannot understand until you
love me? Or someone I mustn't have until I love
you?*
The little girl who hates coffee, the youth who
despises her, or the weary soul who questions
herself.

No Candles Calling Home

This frigid house shivers goosebumps from
the breath of two minus-one.
Burning fireworks cackled in each room of
our humble hovel.
Said light a candle in the window to see,
a vision,
guiding my traveler home from the maze
garden.

Scratching a match, tempted to burn it all
down,
two nails chipped, snatching the candle up.
Lemon citrus battles dust bunnies's odor in
the window,
burning,
The drapes might catch.

You, my second breath, an exhausted promise
found only in the trenches
You, my traveler, an albino bird dipping its
feathers in rainbow hypocrisy.

You, my rock, a strangling subduction zone.
You, my enigma, a track meet without a
starting gun or line of finish.
Me, the blackened night sky, casting the past
millennia guiding the migratory.

Empty, this house is a gopher hole in a barren
field.
A dimming specter saunters, humming
hallowed hymns for
Him,
Burning candles of lemon wax,
Wick seared down,
She, blackened.

Tonight there will be warmth from the breath
of one.
Tonight there will be no lemons,
there will be rigid wax.
Tonight there will be rigid wax.
Tonight there will be no blackened wick,
Hoarse hymns have huffed it out.

What Happens Next?

On occasion, viscous syrup covers the eyes,
driving the unrepentant memory inward for
wayward emotions to seize hold.

Shriveled up behind the eyes, my essence
floats in a memory, a feeling, with the hand
position of a dancing partner.

It forces me into a slow blitzing waltz,
therefore sinking its teeth deeper with every
spin, as the sultry syrup plugs my nose and
suckles sweeter down my throat.

Drip,
Step,
Gone.

Enraptured, I don't want to flee if this is what
it means to be encompassed.
First, it was memories bursting, weeping with
sentiments.

Then it was muted minutes with sorrow and
furious wings. Location changes became
echoes of what I felt.

Now tangoing with me at random is a bereft
whisper masquerading as love.
Lovely liar it is nothing but the loss of an
imagined entanglement.

Smothered in syrup, I'm forced to remember:
I buried you. Not the liar, but the one who
believed the lies.

Snapping from the trappings of sugary
remembrance, what happens now? I'm not
waiting, nor obsessed.

What happens now?

Sleepless Twilight

12 o'clock, man it's late, ugh midnight.
    1 o'clock, okay, okay.
        2 o'clock, does this count as
tomorrow or yesterday?

3 o'clock, guess these bags are here to stay,
haha.
    4 o'clock, damn it, why I am still
awake!
        5 o'clock, eyes scorched by
screens that refuse to fade to black.

6 o'clock, sunrise bleeds through the back.
    7 o'clock, wish time would rewind.
        8 o'clock, guess it's time for
me to force the drop.

9 o'clock, knocked-dropped dead to the Earth.
    1 o'clock, jumping alert.
        2 o'clock, unfocused–sluggish
at work.

3 o'clock, classes carry my hearse around
campus.
4 o'clock, you expect me to learn,
scribbled notes flow before they float away.
5 o'clock, finally, on my way
home!

6 o'clock, this bed is the best thing I own.
7 o'clock, what am I doing? I need to
get in the zone.
8 o'clock, breadsticks, first
meal of the day, delicious.

9 o'clock, damn I wish to thrust it away, hope
it dies and quickly starts to decay.
10 o'clock, maybe I'll try harder today.
11 o'clock, wait... is it me, or
just a bad way?

12 o'clock, midnight, man, it's late.

Under Pressure

Name scrawled above the dotted line. The due
date is not far behind.
Erase. Cross-out. Repeat. Rewind.
What was the question? What was the answer?
Where even am I?

Piecing together fragmented information.
Was it always broken, or was it just the way I
wrote it?
Scribbled notes floating. Ink smears ruin my
clothing.

Eraser shavings stick to my shirt, removing
bad fashion omens.
Polka dot socks, tie-dye shirt, high-waisted
jeans,
Undershirt barely concealing what's
underneath,

A bra would help but there isn't one clean,
Too busy to do the laundry,
Too lazy to take them downstairs,

Too tired—these shorts can take another
week,
No, they can't.
Up all night, sweat got me beat.

Smelling like old shoes in the summer heat.
Need a shower, but this gel doesn't feel like
it's doing anything.
Hair mousse running low, therefore frizzy
curls.

Need to spend some money.
Mama calling again.
*How's it going? What did you do? Have you called
them yet? Got a job?*

Filling out applications left and right,
Editing my resume feels like somebody else's
life.
Who is that?

Where'd they go?
I did that?
No! No! No!

I used to have fun,
Friends asked me out,
Friends wanted to go out tonight,

To another party.
Where I take them home because I put up a
fight.
No weed, no jungle juice, no hit for me.

Substances might make it better but it's the
crash,
The fall apart, the headaches, the vomiting,
Takes too much.

Instead, I indulge in another addiction.
Netflix, Hulu, Amazon, VRV, Disney+, and
HBO Max help me calm my nerves.
Click on Peacock, Tubi, find another movie.

Relive my childhood, when everything was
easy.
Nothing trying to trip me up,
Nobody trying to wear me out,

No self-doubt,

No procrastination,
No pressure from within to keep me awake
when I should be sleeping,

No pressure to put me to sleep when I should
be working.

Scatterbrain

Cannot help these emotions growing,
overflowing,
coursing inside of me.

Uprooted spot,
Put up a mailbox claiming permanent
residency.

Making themselves known when they come to
collect from me,
Rent.

As if this is not my home,
They are an interloping guest that should be
afraid of me.

Daunted by these endless possibilities.
Piercing the mind, seeping inside, and pulling
down pride before leaving me broken inside.

FAILURE!

The alarm, the ring, the hum,
My mind,

Keeps me awake at night.
Insomnia is feasting to devour me alive.

Slow to speak because my mouth is not as fast
as my mind.
They don't understand most times I just want
to get lost and hide.

Doctors try to diagnose me with ADHD, but
that's not fine.
It explains why my conclusions twist other
minds.

The thread, the strings that pull these lines,
The web I weave is far from undefined,

I'm just so lost, the real me is hard to find.
Wade through my darkness.

Wish you could see through my bloodshot
eyes.

Every positive is negative even when the
negative flips on its side.
Too afraid to fail.
Terrified to leave behind the person I was,

She was the only light,
Brittle and frail she soared to great heights,

But flying is dangerous when all you see are
kites.
Caught up in wind patterns from left to right.

So every time I pick up a pen,
It quickly turns into something dark and
depressing.

This storm is harsh but I've never known a
better life,
So what, I'm not the best sister, the best
daughter, the best friend, or the best woman.

I don't give a shit!
Too busy conducting the voices inside.

Cards of Life

All my life, I envisioned I was a princess;
turns out I'm Cinderella, without the mice
and the magic Auntie, scrubbing floors as my
nails chip and my fingers scream: crack, crack,
crack, deeper than the Grand Canyon. Arid
patches left potholes; all my life I envisioned I
was a princess, dressed in the brightest pinks
and blues, a tasteful mini-skirt and jean jacket
too; what I see now, I didn't know then:
Goodwill, Factory 2 You, Pay for Less, with
off-brand and seasoned cheap foods: chicken,
beans, and rice kept me fed with my mattress
topper on the floor, sheetless; turns out I've
always been Cinderella working twice as
hard, *Clean those dishes—*
excuses build bridges to nowhere; *Scrub those
baseboards* life is not about how hard you get
hit; *Move those clothes—*be the labor great or
small; *Run faster,* have faith; *Get a job*; the tale
of betrayal follows the illusion of security,
thinking the rug was stable beneath my feet,
no matter the quakes and shakes I believed;
it's clear to me my princess gown was made to

keep me asleep, to blind from the truth; *where
did these rags come from?*, thought I was your
little girl, your princess; *why are there holes in
these seams?*; you want me to learn how to fix
them, to walk a mile in your shoes to
understand; how you've failed me, yourself,
and all your forgotten plans
I own over twenty pairs of shoes and I still
don't want to wear them; still transfixed in
the place I've always been, a card in your deck
to play, hold, or bluff.

Destructive Sight

When I was young, back before the sun rose, the sound of drums switched from easy mode and put me on the roaming path. Inching up before brothers, coming up on fields, stretching up for gold, like Douglas and Biles, I wanted it all. Around the bend, I saw it clear as day. My Mamma foretold I would succeed from the day I was born.

For years, I kept trucking, keeping my head above the crowd, watching people I passed fall. Eyes up, no time to die. Failure is something I cannot let happen; it's unacceptable. It's a path filled with many attractions.

Yes, depression is a blanket I drown wrapped in. A smile is nothing more than a frown's best try at acting. Monotonous days fly by as I'm spiraling, fighting something that's been built up inside. It creeps around until you look up, everything is floating, but you. You sink to the bottom, sticky goo; feet

stuck, Chuck, you're my favorite pair, but it
might be time to lose.
Don't know how I'm going to get on by, this
barefoot trek leaves bloody and paralyzed.

      Can't voice problems, can't voice pain.
Keeping it all inside, arching my back insane.
When I open up I hear voices saying they
know. But no, we are not the same, you have
no idea the troubles I tame, with one falter
they are set aflame. Screaming telling me I'm
the only one to blame.

Taunting, *Where is your faith?* Think you
should change your name. So in this endless
battle, I collect arrows and pray for better
aim. Calling on the same strength Jesus was
known to claim. Thirsting to be held by God's
frame, lift my head, I was born to be
unashamed.

A Canopy

Rushing over me, this tsunami, not knowing
when this tempest will ever cease.
Rushing over me, the waves I endure; my
spirit has a canopy of defense.

Rain overhead, seeping into my shoulders, are
blessings and favor.
Standing straighter these waters will boil
beneath my feet revealing a path of dry land.

A path of righteous glory where my grip is
strong, my sword is unbreakable.

Feminine Nature

I'm the type of woman who knows she's a woman but doesn't know when it happened. This change from innocent baby, to scabbed up tomboy, to growing breasts preteen, to virginal young lady, finally to legally a woman. I'm a woman of lucky shape, yet I watch other figures and my weights.

I'm the type of woman who loves animation, cartoons, and comics. Harsh print of both color, black and white, and blank where love builds bridges, where characters create obstacles for themselves, where color palettes convey feelings. I'm a woman who plunges headfirst, quickly, yet ennui wades not far behind.

I'm the type of woman who excels at inspiring others meanwhile ignoring the change my inspiration will bring. Piling blanket upon blanket to hide me from family, friends, demons, my actions from God. I'm a sinful woman seeking redemption, yet I know I will sin again.

I'm the type of woman who desires
love, dreams of love, but chases loneliness
from a distaste, distrust, disdain of real love.
Squeezing a grudge into my favorite mug, the
mug of a woman who looks like me, a black
woman, beautifully bitter to drink until it
mixes with the blue in my veins poisoning me.
I'm an easy woman to love yet not easy to
please.

I'm the type of woman who has
perfected humility married to self-doubt. In
society it is not polite to gloat about oneself,
to acknowledge your brilliance, to believe in
yourself. I'm a woman who knows the passion
is there, yet I still question for reassurance.

I'm the type of woman who consumes
traits, complaints, pleasurable praises.
Permeating through layers of thick
transparent skin until I'm bloated enough to
profess I don't mind woes cast upon my curly
head.

I'm the type of woman who knows she
is a woman and knows what to do with that.

Floating Troubles

O' sweet child of mine, take courage,
Heed not the doubts of unbelievers.

O' sweet child of mine embrace love,
A wanting for love is most right.

O' sweet child of mine, float troubles.
Seeping in cleansing.

O' sweet child of mine prepare armor,
Polished and waxed your foes will be blinded.

O' sweet child of mine display sympathy,
Your eyes may not perceive, so let your heart
prevail.

O' sweet child of mine breathe easy,
All things are possible.

O' sweet child of mine, demand focus,
Palpitations and bleeding hearts distract.

O' sweet child of mine walk with joy,
Each footfall is a promise fulfilled.

O' sweet child of mine you are,
Beautiful.

Four Women

Woolly, w, oo, ll, y; woolly.

W, *who has this woolly hair?* Those who are
black, yellow, tan, and brown.
Brothers and sisters adorn crowns of wool in
locs, braids, curls, afros, and coils.

Oo, only us for eternity, that double vowel is
a symbol of infinity, the everlasting relation
with wool.

L, it is lonely four-textured hair, it is
something we have, but don't share.
L, it is lovely four-textured hair, a lovely
hassle, but lovely nonetheless.

Y, yes it can be described as woolly, yet it isn't
always convenient, yes it is apart from
everyone else's tresses, but yes it is yours, yes
it is extraordinary, yes I hope you love woolly
hair,

I do!

A Summer of Tears

We thought there was going to be change,
nothing was going to stay the same; got a
Black president filled with hope for a future
where people might finally pronounce our
names; then we had a new man with a red hat
filled with hard lies, false promises stacked
sky, sitting in our Oval Office popping pills
while the rest of us sat and died; got anger in
the streets, got lies in the streets, got pride in
the streets, got people in the streets screaming
for the people who died in the streets, hoping
for a better life in these streets; protect and
serve, nah cops got to protect their nerves, we
have to respect their words, *Yes sir, No sir*;
hands-on the dash I'm scared to pull it out
even if they ask; *riot, riot, everybody riot!*;
nothing ever gets done in silence; hold my
breath, can't they got pressure on my chest,
hoping if I'm quiet they can move on to who's
next; back to back and back again the same
old Karen calls the cops again; boxed in, six
by eight, *What I'd do?*; they said I was breaking
into my own home, or was I out running

again for my life against those, they'll never convict; *Who am I?*; just another person who's sick, fed up the lies they feed since you lay in the crib; *Where am I?*; living in the thick of it, *Why am I?*; feeling so tired of it because they say things are getting better while we fill the family crypt, *How am I?*; going to deal with it, pray to God before I raise my fists.

Turgid Sea

Holding my history on the bow of a ship.
Washing blood from a skinned knee,
Seeing for the first time,
Black sand, white sand,
Different degrees,
Eroding rock obscuring details from behind
island trees,
Reach deep, uncovering spiraling shells
hiding beings,
In with the surf putrid smelling green,
At high tide mixed with rubbish,
The sea holds my history, but sunk I know not
where,
Until it arrives on this shore,
Smoothed and massaged by raging force,
Bleached by the unyielding sun,
Revealed by the receding wave,
Before it's cast aback.

Founding Struggle

Atop their bones seed this country,
     Command it to grow!
Echos of their tears haunt the westward
wind,
Bare feet deep in soil
With backs hunched over to toil,
     Bring them hither! Fetter them and their
litter!
A price on their head is another soul bought
aboard,
Strip and add stripes if they cause strife,
Property is their right as the bartered and
owned,

Welcome thieves! Welcome religious! Welcome
persecuted! Welcome uneducated! Welcome all!

This land is yours to own through
citizenship,
A bayonet,
Torn apart by privileged frets this country
must overcome the dividing,
Multiplying minority threat.

Freedom for you! Freedom for all!

Silence for those three-fifths and the skins
stuck on reserve,
Toiling for hours to lay the track used to
steamroll what little they have left,
Give them ghettos, small towns, and little
neighborhoods,
They are welcome to fight for scraps while the
money accrues out of their depth.

Saddled with bootstraps they will work to
mount the horse, but without soles, they slip,
Slither in the clay.
Upright they sit and march astride, while
mine are under hoof.